Contents

People in the story

Ebenezer
Scrooge

Bob
Cratchit

Marley's
ghost

The Ghost
of Christmas
Past

The Ghost
of Christmas
Present

The Ghost
of Christmas
Future

New words

chain

clerk

ghost

poor

rich

turkey

Note about the story

Charles Dickens (1812–1870) was an English writer. His family were **poor***. He had to leave school at the age of twelve and work for ten hours a day. But Dickens started writing, and he became **rich** and famous. He wrote *A Christmas Carol* in 1843.

In England at that time, there were lots of very poor people. In *A Christmas Carol*, Dickens shows that we must be nice to our families, and that we must help poor people.

Before-reading questions

1 What do English people do at Christmas? Are these sentences *true* or *false*? Write your answers in your notebook.
   a They eat turkey.
   b They work hard.
   c They are with their families.
   d They eat chocolate eggs.

2 Look at the "People in the story" on page 4. Choose two people, and describe them. Here are some ideas.
   • He is wearing . . .
   • He looks about . . . years old.
   • He looks happy/sad.
   • He is/isn't nice.

*Definitions of words in **bold** can be found in the glossary on pages 62–63.

CHAPTER ONE
Marley's ghost

London, 1843

Jacob Marley is **dead**.

This was Marley's office.

This is Ebenezer Scrooge, Marley's **partner**.
He is **rich**, but he has a cold **heart**.

This is Scrooge's **clerk**, Bob Cratchit.
He is **poor**, but he has a warm heart.

A boy sings a Christmas **carol** for money.

Listen! Three ghosts are coming to your house: the first tomorrow at 1 a.m.; the second the next night at 1 a.m.; and the third the next night at 12 a.m.

CHAPTER TWO
The first ghost

Marley told me about three ghosts. Are you the first?

Yes. I am the Ghost of Christmas **Past**. Your past.

The second ghost

They are at Bob Cratchit's house.

The third ghost

This is the dead man. I understand – I must look. But I don't want to. Let's go. I am scared!

They go to Bob Cratchit's house.

Where is your father?
He is **late**.

Father walks slowly now.
He walked very fast with Tiny Tim.
He loved him, and he was happy.

Father is here.

The end

What can I do now? I don't know. But I am very happy!

Little boy, what day is it?

Today? It's Christmas Day, of course.

Oh, good!

Listen. Do you know the shop in the next street? There is a very big **turkey** in that shop. Go and buy it. Send it to Bob Cratchit's house. Merry Christmas!

Merry Christmas.

Scrooge is at Fred's house.

The family eat turkey and play games.

The next morning, Scrooge is at his office.

Oh, good. Bob is late.

Good morning, Mr Scrooge.

Scrooge changed. He lived a good life. Scrooge was a second father to Tiny Tim.

Scrooge never saw the ghosts again, but he remembered their lessons.

During-reading questions

Write the answers to these questions in your notebook.

CHAPTER ONE

1 Why does the little boy sing a carol?
2 Who was Jacob Marley?
3 Why does Jacob Marley have a chain?

CHAPTER TWO

1 Are these sentences *true* or *false*?
   a The Ghost of Christmas Past thinks Scrooge is a really good person.
   b The Ghost of Christmas Past and Scrooge go to Scrooge's past.
   c Scrooge sees his old town, and he is sad.
   d The boy sitting alone in the classroom (on page 23) is Scrooge.
2 Old Fezziwig makes people happy. How?
3 Scrooge doesn't marry the young woman (on page 25). Why not?

CHAPTER THREE

1 Who says "I see an empty chair in the future."?
2 Are the people living in the hut (on page 34) rich?

CHAPTER FOUR

1 Two people are dead in this chapter. Who are they?
2 Are these people dead in the present or in the future?
3 What does Scrooge think of Christmas at the end of Chapter Four?

1 There is a mistake in every sentence. Correct the mistakes in your notebook.

   a Scrooge thinks he can't change.

   b Scrooge is happy because the ghosts are there.

   c It is New Year's Day.

   d Scrooge tells the boy to buy the Cratchit family a goose.

   e Fred is sad to see his uncle.

   f Scrooge lived a bad life.

   g Tiny Tim died.

After-reading questions

1 Why did the ghosts come?

2 Look at all the poor people in the book. How can you see they are poor?

3 At the beginning of the story, Scrooge has a cold heart. At the end of the story, Scrooge is a good person. When does this change begin?

4 Who is your favourite person in the story? Why?

5 Can you learn from the three ghosts? Can you be a better person? How can you change?

Exercises

1 Complete these sentences in your notebook. Use the
present simple form of the verbs in brackets. Sometimes,
you must make the verb negative.

1 Jacob Marley ....*is*............... (be) dead.

2 Bob Cratchit .... (be) rich.

3 Fred .... (say) "Merry Christmas and a Happy New Year, Bob!"

4 Scrooge .... (give) money to poor people.

5 Scrooge says that ghosts .... (be) real.

2 Complete these sentences in your notebook, using the
words from the box.

partner	children	clerk	uncle	wife

1 Jacob Marley was Scrooge's ....*partner*..........

2 Bob Cratchit is Scrooge's ....

3 Scrooge is Fred's ....

4 Bob Cratchit has a ....

5 Bob Cratchit also has lots of ....

CHAPTER TWO

3 Match the words to their meanings. Write the correct
answers in your notebook.

Example: 1 – c

1 fantastic   **a** Christmas song

2 marry   **b** begin

3 carol   **c** very good

4 different   **d** not the same

5 start   **e** be husband and wife

4 Complete the sentences in your notebook using the words from the box.

| carol | different | looks | marry | start |

1 A boy came to Scrooge's office last night and sang a Christmas ....*carol*..............

2 Fezziwig says the Christmas party can .... now.

3 Scrooge .... sad.

4 Scrooge and the woman can't .... because Scrooge is .... now.

CHAPTER THREE

5 Complete these sentences in your notebook with the correct adjective. Use the letters in brackets.

1 The Cratchit family are ....*poor*............ (oopr).

2 The Ghost of Christmas Present's torch doesn't give .... (chri) people happiness.

3 Bob Cratchit and his family are .... (yhpap) together.

4 Tiny Tim is not .... (elwl).

CHAPTER FOUR

6 Complete these sentences in your notebook.

1 The Ghost of Christmas Futures comes. Scrooge is very ....*scared*.......... of him.

2 Three men talk about a dead man. They say he died last ....

3 A woman took the .... from the dead man's bed.

4 Bob Cratchit walks slowly because .... is dead, and he is sad.

7 Complete these sentences in your notebook, using the correct prepositions from the box.

at	from	on	for	in	of

1 The Ghost of Christmas Future comes ....*at*.......... 12 a.m.
2 Scrooge is very scared .... this ghost.
3 .... the future, Tiny Tim is dead.
4 Scrooge buys a turkey .... the Cratchit family.
5 .... Christmas Day, Scrooge goes to Fred's house.
6 Scrooge learns a lot .... the ghosts.

8 Complete these sentences in your notebook. Use the past simple of the verbs in brackets.

1 Jacob Marley ....*died*............ (die) in 1836.
2 A boy .... (sing) a carol at Scrooge's office.
3 Scrooge .... (give) him nothing.
4 Scrooge never .... (marry).
5 The Cratchit children .... (see) their goose in the shop.
6 A woman .... (take) the shirt from the dead man's body.
7 A man .... (pay) her some money for the shirt.
8 Scrooge .... (be) a second father to Tiny Tim.

Project work

1 You are Ebenezer Scrooge. Fred is interviewing you.
   Answer the questions in your notebook.
   Fred: Hello, Uncle. Three ghosts came to your house! Wow!
        Were you scared?
   Scrooge: ....
   Fred: What were the names of the ghosts?
   Scrooge: ....
   Fred: What did the first ghost show you?
   Scrooge: ....
   Fred: Oh, really? And the second ghost?
   Scrooge: ....
   Fred: OK. And the third ghost?
   Scrooge: ....
   Fred: That's scary! You didn't like Christmas. But, now, you
        love it! Why?
   Scrooge: ....
   Fred: Now, you are a good person. You do lots of kind
        things. What good things do you do?
   Scrooge: ....
   Fred: That is great. Thank you for talking to me, Uncle.
        Merry Christmas!

2 Write a story about a Scrooge-like person in your notebook.
   Who are they?

3 There are many films of *A Christmas Carol*. Do you know any
   of them? Are they very different from the book? How are
   they different?

An answer key for all questions and exercises can be found at
www.penguinreaders.co.uk

Glossary

alone (adj.)
You have no one with you.

Bah! Humbug!
(interjection + n.)
(old English) Scrooge says this
because he is angry.

carol (n.)
a Christmas song

chain (n.)
You put a *chain* around things
and animals. Then they cannot
move.

change (v.)
(1) When a thing *changes*, it
starts to be different.
(2) When a person *changes*, they
start to be different. In this
story, Scrooge *changes* and starts
to be a nice person.

clerk (n.)
A *clerk* works in an office.

curtains (n.)
You put *curtains* in front of
windows or around a bed.

dead (adj.)
not living

empty (adj.)
An *empty* thing has nothing in it.
An *empty* chair has no one on it.

fantastic (adj.)
very good

future (n.)
the time after now (for example,
tomorrow, next week, next year)

ghost (n.)
In stories, people die and come
back as *ghosts*. *Ghosts* are
not living.

Go away! (phr. v. – imperative)
You say "*Go away*" because you
want a person to go.

goose (n.)
a big bird. People sometimes
eat a *goose* at Christmas. In this
story, the *goose* is small.

happiness (n.)
when you are happy

heart (n.)
A person with a cold *heart* does
not want to help other people.

kind (adj.)
A *kind* person wants to help
other people.

late (adj.)
after the right time

life (n.)
from the beginning of living, to the end of living. This is a *life*.

marry (v.)
to start to be husband and wife, or husband and husband, or wife and wife

partner (n.)
You work with a *partner*.

past (n.)
the time before now

poor (adj.)
Poor people do not have much money.

present (n.)
The *present* is now.

real (adj.)
Real things are true, and you can see them.

rich (adj.)
A *rich* person has a lot of money.

scared (adj.)
You are *scared* because maybe something bad can happen to you.

torch (n.)
a long thing with fire or a light at its end. You carry it when it is dark.

turkey (n.)
a big bird. People eat *turkey* at Christmas. In this story, people pay a lot of money for a *turkey*.

uncle (n.)
the brother of your mother or father (for example, Uncle Scrooge)

Penguin **Readers**

Visit **www.penguinreaders.co.uk**
for FREE Penguin Readers resources
and digital and audio versions of this book.